SUM

MW01504688

THE POWER OF

NOW

▬ ▬ ▬ ▬ ▬ ▬ ▬

BOOK-NOTE GIFTS

TABLE OF CONTENTS

Introduction

The Power of Now: A Guide to Spiritual Enlightenment requires us to bid adieu to our analytical mind and its deceptively formed self; the ego. We need to step into the spiritual and approach the book by entering a higher place, where the air is spiritual or higher. We will learn that we are not the same as our mind. If we succumb to the Now, we can discover true human power. The body, silence and the space in our surroundings can all serve as keys to the Now. These access points can help us reach the Now, which is free from problems.

We can discover joy and welcome our true selves in the present moment. We also find that we are whole and perfect. We will discover that our most significant barrier to this realization is our relationships, particularly our intimate relationships. We will learn that if we utilize our relationships cleverly, they can serve as an entrance to spiritual enlightenment. We can benefit from our relationships to be more conscious and caring human beings. It can establish a true spiritual union between us and others.

If we learn to be completely present and move toward the Now, if we start comprehending the truth of the words "forgiveness",

"Unmanifested", "inner-body" and "surrender", we can enter The Power of Now.

Preface

This book falls into the category of those books that are actually alive in a sense of the word and can transform people's lives. This book has successfully changed, pleased and healed people. The author's teachings welcome the core of every religion and do not go against them.

Foreword

Russell E. DiCarlo sheds several myths in the foreword and underlines that contrary to popular belief, humanity has not arrived at the zenith of its development, we are indeed connected with one another, the universe and nature, and there is a world beyond the physical external we witness.

Background: The Roots of the Book

The author recalls his life before 30. He experienced continual anxiety and occasional suicidal depression. One day after turning 29, the author woke up with a feeling of intense terror. He realized that he could not live with himself like this. He further pondered whether he was two different entities, both 'he' and 'himself.' What followed was five months of ecstasy and peace. He realized several years later that he had experienced something truly remarkable that day. He comprehended that his suffering that night had reached a point that it caused his consciousness to pull out from its identification of the sad and extremely frightened self, which is nothing except for the fabricated works of the mind.

Withdrawal from What Does Not Matter

The extraction had been so comprehensive that it caused the fake, agonizing self to crumble fully. It left only the author's true nature as the persistent 'I am': the pure state of consciousness before its classification with form. The author was able to achieve an even higher level of bliss and purity later. He had nothing physical left including no home, relationships and job. He had no social identity.

Even though this phase lasted for two years and had to come to an end, the peace he experienced then still lives within him and manifests itself in different forms.

When people ask Eckhart Tolle to give them what he has, he tells them that they already have it within themselves; they just cannot recognize it since their mind is talking too much. Eventually, Tolle finally had an external presence again and became a spiritual teacher.

The Truth that Simmers within Us

This book answers the several questions Tolle has been asked by people over the years. It offers the essence of his teachings. The discourse of the book switches between two levels throughout. Tolle uses one level to direct the readers' attention to the false inside them. He utilizes the second level to shed light on the insightful change of our consciousness. It is possible for everyone regardless of who and where they are. Tolle teaches us the way to liberate ourselves from being a slave of the mind, reach the enlightened state of consciousness and maintain it all the time.

Chapter 1: You Are Different from Your Mind

The Biggest Barrier to Enlightenment

Those of us who have not discovered their real wealth, which is the glowing joy of Being and the invincible feeling of peace that accompanies it, are beggars regardless of their material possessions. We are trying to derive pleasure from external sources even though there is true wealth within us. This treasure outshines everything else in the world.

Definition of Enlightenment

Enlightenment is not something larger than life. It is just our real state of felt singleness with Being. It entails discovering our real nature away from form and name. Buddha defines enlightenment as the eradication of suffering.

Definition of Being

Being is the everlasting One Existence other than the innumerable forms of life that experience birth and death. Being does not just outdo but also exists deep inside all forms as their deepest, unconquerable and imperishable crux. You can access it now since it is your own inmost self. However, avoid trying to use your mind to comprehend it. You can only become aware of it if your mind is silent. When you dedicate your attention to the Now completely and passionately and are present, you can feel Being but cannot ever fully comprehend it.

If Being means God, why Doesn't the Author Use the Word God?

Tolle explains that he uses Being instead of God because a lot of people misuse the word God. They associate a mental image with God. This is not the case with the word Being. It is free from people's possession or complications. Being is open and infinite. Being is reachable to us as a part of us.

The Biggest Barrier to Experiencing this Reality

What stands between us and Being is our tendency to think all the time. It stops us from accessing the inner tranquility that is intertwined with Being. Thinking has turned into an illness. The mind is extremely productive if we utilize it correctly. However, it can be damaging if we utilize it incorrectly.

Avoid Being a Slave of Your Mind

If you believe that you cannot stop thinking even briefly, then you have become a slave of your mind. When you accept that you are not the thinker, it takes you toward freedom and triggers a higher level of consciousness. Keep an eye on the thinker. You will comprehend that thought is a very small component of intelligence.

Untangle Yourself from Your Mind

There is a voice or voices inside all our heads. These are the unintentional thought processes that we do not know that we can put a stop to. These unfold in the form of ongoing monologues or dialogues.

However, we have the ability to unshackle ourselves from our mind. We can begin this very moment. Listen to the voice in your head as much as you can. Pay heed to recurrent thought patterns. This is what Tolle means when he says 'watch the thinker.'

Do not be biased while listening to the voice. Avoid judging it. You will feel that you are listening to it. When you realize this, you will understand that this sense of your presence is not a thought. It stems from somewhere beyond the mind.

When you hear a thought, your awareness includes both the thought and your position as its witness. This means that your consciousness now has a new dimension. When you hear the thought, you experience a mindful existence. This is your profound self, below the thought.

As a thought dwindles, a break happens in the mental stream. This gap is called "no-mind." These gaps start increasing in their magnitude with time. They come with a lot of peace and harmony. This is the start of your experienced oneness with Being. When you proceed further in this state of no-mind, you start experiencing pure consciousness.

An Alternate Practice

You can also try introducing a break in the mind stream by channeling your focus and concentrating on the Now rather than 'watching the thinker.' Be extremely aware of the current moment.

Enlightenment: Going Beyond Thought

We keep thinking about either the past or the future. We should focus on the present. Our freedom is connected to the current moment. No-mind allows creativity to unfold.

Emotion: The Body's Response to the Mind

Our mind is not limited to thoughts only. It also entails our emotions and other mental-emotional responsive patterns. Emotions appear at the junction where mind and body come together. It is the body's response to the mind or an echo of our mind. Powerful emotions can alter the biochemistry of the body. An attack thought will cause us to experience the emotion of anger.

If you identify a lot with your thinking, inclinations, aversions, rulings and elucidations, or in other words, if you are not present as the observing consciousness to a substantial degree, your emotional energy charge will be powerful. If you isolate yourself from your emotions, you will gradually go through your emotions on a completely physical level. This will unfold as a physical symptom or issue.

If you cannot feel your emotions easily, concentrate on the energy field inside your body. This will bring you closer to your emotions. Emotion watching is as critical as thought watching. Avoid analyzing, only observe.

Positive Emotions: Love and Joy

They are closely connected to our natural state of getting interlinked with Being. When we experience a gap in our thought stream, we can experience indications of love or joy or instants of peace.

How to Handle Cravings and Pain

Cravings are born when our mind tries to accomplish contentment or salvation in external things or in the future as a replacement of the joy of Being. Avoid trying to free yourself from desire or accomplish 'enlightenment.' Be present and watch your mind.

All of us experience pain. A relationship that gives us joy can very easily turn into one that gives us pain. Our pain has two levels. One is the pain we generate now. The second one is the past pain that still occupies our mind and body. We need to put a halt to the creation of current pain and evaporate past pain.

Key Lesson

The most significant step toward enlightenment is to learn to detach oneself from one's mind. The power of your consciousness will become stronger with the formation of every single gap in your mind stream.

Chapter 2: Consciousness: Your Ticket to Freedom from Pain

Stop Giving Rise to Pain in the Present

We might think that since everyone experiences pain and grief, we should learn to coexist with them instead of trying to steer clear of them. However, a substantial portion of our pain is unneeded. We create it ourselves when we are not watching our mind and letting it control our life.

The pain we form now is a kind of deviation from acceptance. It is a type of unconscious opposition to what exists. As far as the level of thought goes, this resistance acts like a type of judgment. As far as the level of emotion goes, it unfolds as a type of negativity. The severity of the pain relies on how strongly you are battling the current moment. This further relies on the degree to which you are branded with your mind. The mind continuously tries to evade the Now and those who identify a lot with their minds suffer. On the other hand, when you truly accept the Now, it will free you from your pain and suffering.

Why Does the Mind Reject the Now?

It does so because it cannot work and stay in control without time, which includes past and future, so it considers the timeless Now to be intimidating. We cannot separate mind and time. The mind keeps covering up the Now with past and future to sustain its control, which causes the boundless creative potential of Being to be hidden by time. Being cannot be isolated from the Now. This causes your real nature to be buried by the mind.

How to Avoid Pain

If you do not want to give rise to any more pain for yourself and other people, and if you do not wish to multiply the past pain within yourself, then do not produce any more time, other than what you require to handle your life's practical aspects.

How to Avoid Creating Time

To avoid creating more time, understand that you only have the present moment. Focus on the Now as the most significant thing. Make Now your permanent residence and only visit past and future when the pragmatic aspects of your life require it. Embrace life since Now is everything. Succumb to it. You will see your life transform.

What If the Present Moment is Terrible?

Our mind labels the present moment as terrible and judges it so that we can avoid it. This creates pain and sorrow. Get rid of your mind's resistance and let the current moment be. This will bring you closer to inner freedom and peace.

Accept what the current moment has to offer as if you selected it. Function with it and turn it into a friend. It will significantly change your life.

Getting Rid of Past Pain

Our past pain accumulates in our mind since childhood. This pain serves as a negative energy field that engulfs our mind and body. It is the emotional pain - body and its two modes include active and inactive. Some of us experience our pain-body in particular circumstances only while others are always living through it.

Some pain-bodies are harmless. Others can be violent or intense. Some lead to accidents or diseases. Others can cause people to attempt suicide.

If a pain-body is opening within you, watch it. It can turn into annoyance, rage and other things. It might cause you to try to add drama to your relationship. Respond to it when it tries to switch from its dormant state. The pain-body wishes to survive by making you identify with it. If it takes control of you, you will desire more pain and become a victim.

If you watch the pain-body as an observer, you have become free from its power and embraced the Now.

What Happens When We Become Sufficiently Conscious to Smash Our Identification with a Pain-Body?

When we become watchers of the pain - body, the pain - body will continue to operate for some time and will try to make us identify with it again. We need to stay alert and conscious.

The Ego and its Identification with the Pain-Body

When you try to sever your identification with the pain-body, you will face inner resistance. This will especially be strong if you have spent a significant part of your life staying identified with the pain - body. You will experience an unconscious dread of losing your identity. Stay vigilant. Watch the satisfaction you get from being sad. You are the only one who can achieve this.

Where Does Fear Come From?

We avoid putting our hand in the fire because we are aware that it will get burned if we do so. Fear is not what we need to steer clear of unneeded danger. We just need basic intelligence and common sense for that.

The psychological condition of fear has no link with real danger. It has many forms including phobia, nervousness, dread, anxiety, worry and others. This type of psychological fear focuses on the possibility of something happening instead of something happening now. You are living in the now while your mind is in the future. This leads to an anxiety gap. If you identify with your mind and do not comprehend the straightforward nature of the Now, that anxiety gap will never leave you alone. You can handle the Now but not the future. Additionally, when you keep identifying with your mind, your ego will run your life.

The ego is always uncertain and feels threatened. This is true even when it seems confident on the surface. The ego will keep sending the message of danger and threat to the body. This ongoing message will give rise to the emotion of fear.

Types of Fear

Fear is of several types but the ego's fear of death drives all fears. The ego considers death to be always imminent. The ego thinks that being wrong equals dying. This has caused so many wars in the past.

When you have isolated yourself from your mind, your sense of self will have nothing to do with being right or wrong anymore. Your violent desire to be right will not exist any longer. You will not be hostile anymore while sharing your thoughts or feelings. A more profound and real place inside you will give rise to your sense of self, rather than your mind.

Ego's Quest for Completeness

The ego feels incomplete and craves wholeness. It runs after money, success, appreciation, possessions, etc. However, even after achieving these things, the hole is still there because these things are not what actually matters.

Key Lesson

Those who are identified with their mind and detached from their real power, which is their deeper self with its foundation in Being, they will be continually gripped by fear. Almost everyone we meet has some degree of fear. It can range from anxiety or dread to ambiguous discomfort and a detached sense of risk. People notice it only when it becomes prominent. If the egoic mind regulates your life, you will never find peace and will experience a craving for one thing or another.

Chapter 3: Transitioning Further into the Now

Avoid Trying to Find Yourself in Your Mind

You might wish to explore yourself further in your mind before embarking on a journey to achieve pure consciousness. However, this will be futile. There is not a lot to comprehend beyond the dysfunctional nature of the mind. The unconscious state entails your identification of the mind, which gives birth to a false self or the ego. This false self is a replacement of your true self that has its foundation in Being.

The ego's needs never end. It feels threatened and defenseless. It is always fearful and wanting something. This is the fundamental dysfunction of the mind and you do not need to explore deeper.

Stop the Time Delusion

If you feel that it is impossible to break your association with the mind, stop the time illusion. Eliminate time from the mind and it will come to a halt, unless you wish to use it. When you identify with your mind, you are imprisoned in time. You will only wish to exist through reminiscence and expectation. You will be obsessed with the past and future and will not just let the current moment be. This happens because the past offers you an identity and the future encompasses the prospect of fulfillment and salvation. This is a mirage.

How Will Life Exist without the Past, Future and Goals?

You might believe that you will not have an identity without the past or goals to look forward to but you are wrong. Life is Now. Now is the only thing that counts for something. It is the only thing that matters. Now is the only thing that can help you release yourself from the boundaries of your mind.

There is Nothing beyond the Now

You might feel that the past has shaped your identity and your future goals determine your present actions but you must consider that everything happens in the Now. Everything that you have ever gone through, done, felt or thought happened in the Now, not outside it. Now is what matters. Nothing can ever happen in the past or future.

How to Enter the Spiritual Dimension and the Power of the Now

All religions tell you to focus on the Now. What stops us from seeing the light of God is time. Avoid rejecting or opposing the present moment. Make it a habit to avoid thinking about the past or future when it is unneeded. Do not focus on the promise of a better future or the anxiety of a worse future. These are illusions. When you understand that you are not present, it will help you become present.

Psychological Time and Clock Time

If you are working toward a goal, you are utilizing clock time. When you become too consumed with the goal, you turn clock time into psychological time. You will not see the Now, the beauty of nature, or anything else around you.

Psychological Time is Madness

Psychological time is a disease. Ideologies such as communism and nationalism have been based on psychological time or the idea that the future is everything, which caused so many people to lose their lives. The end does not justify the means.

Suffering and Negativity Stem from Time

Negativity originates from buildup of psychological time and rejection of the present. When we excessively focus on the future and not on the present, it leads to apprehension, anxiety, strain and agitation. Similarly, when we focus excessively on the past and not on the present, it leads to bitterness, unforgiveness, remorse, fault, grumbles and sadness.

Try to Discover Life beyond Your Circumstances

You might feel that you are surrounded by a lot of problems and are so worried and unhappy that you cannot be happy even if you focus on the Now. However, you need to comprehend that you have these problems in your life 'because' you are worried about the future and not focusing on the present. Your attention is occupied by time completely and you are not paying heed to the Now. Live and focus on the Now and you will not be unhappy anymore. All problems are a mirage of the mind.

Being and the Joy of It

If you wish to find out whether you have become a slave of psychological time, you can check it using a simple method. Ask yourself whether there is lightness, comfort and joy in what you are doing. If your answer is no, then time is occupying the current moment. Life will seem to be a weight or tussle to you. You might not need to switch from what you are doing. You might only need to alter the way you are doing it. Focus on the current moment and the act instead of the outcome. When you respect the current moment, your unease and burden will go away and you will feel light. You will start feeling joy.

Focus on the Action instead of the Result

Do not be concerned about the outcome of your actions. Focus on the action itself. The fruit will follow. You will still be able to concentrate on goals but you will not expect the future to rescue you or bring you joy.

Key Lesson

Do not try to explore your mind. Comprehend its basic dysfunction and be present. Do not let your egoic mind take over your life. Remove time from the mind and it will cease to work over time.

Chapter 4: Strategies Used by the Mind to Evade the Now

The World is Dominated by Time

Even if the world is dominated by time, you can feel alive if you live in the Now. You will not be a slave of time when each cell in your body feels the joy of Being.

How Can I Enjoy Freedom from Time if I Have to Pay My Bills?

These bills are not the issue. Losing the Now is the issue. Losing the Now equals losing Being. To have freedom from time means to have freedom from the psychological desire to hold on to the past for your identity and the future for your contentment. It entails the most intense switch of consciousness ever possible.

Different Levels of Unconsciousness

When most of us are awake, we switch between ordinary and deep unconsciousness. Ordinary unconsciousness entails being linked with your emotions and thought processes, your wants, dislikes and responses. This is the regular state of most people. This means staying ignorant of Being and getting controlled by the egoic mind. It entails constant nervousness, displeasure or apprehension. You might not be aware of it. You will feel relaxed when it comes to a halt. This unease related to ordinary unconsciousness converts into the pain linked with deep unconsciousness. The latter entails more severe suffering or gloom when things do not go the right way.

What Shows Your Unconsciousness Level

What shows your level of consciousness is the way you handle life's challenges. An unconscious person turns more deeply unconscious through these challenges. A conscious person becomes more strongly conscious.

Getting Rid of Ordinary Unconsciousness

Turn it into a conscious thing. Watch the several manners in which strain, displeasure and discomfort unfold because of unneeded judgment, opposition to what is, and rejection of the Now. You can disband anything unconscious by showering the light of consciousness on it. You can also get brighter this way. Track your mental-emotional state by watching yourself.

Liberate Yourself from Unhappiness

If you are unhappy in your job, either stop doing it and find something else or stop being negative about it. Talk to the person in question since negativity serves no purpose. The best way to get rid of negativity is by eliminating it. It is that simple.

Your Life's Purpose

We might end up thinking that our life is supposed to have a purpose. We might think that we would go astray without it. In addition, purpose is linked with the future. So how can we live in the present? The answer is that it definitely helps to know your destination or the direction you are taking. However, what matters most is the step you are taking in the present moment. Your life's journey has both an internal and external purpose. Its external purpose is to reach the goals you have. However, if you completely focus on your destination or the future, you might miss your life's internal purpose. Its internal purpose is not related to your destination or what you are doing. It is related to the way you are doing it. It is concerned with the way your consciousness is at the current moment. Our external purpose matters to us when we have not fulfilled our inner purpose.

Key Lesson

To be free from time means letting go of the psychological need to hold on to your past for your identity and future for your fulfillment. Liberate yourself from time by getting rid of this need. Focus on the Now.

Chapter 5: The State of Presence

What is the State of Presence?

We cannot think about or comprehend the state of presence. We can only be present and that translates into comprehending it. If you stay alert and tell yourself that you are pondering what your next thought is going to be, it will not come quickly.

Stay Strongly Embedded within Yourself

Dwell your body completely. Always pay attention to the internal energy field of your body. Feel the body from within. Being aware of your body will keep you present and in the Now.

What Does Waiting Mean

You have to stay in waiting and this waiting does not mean a bored type of waiting. You have to stay alert, still and vigilant. Anything can happen anytime and if you are not alert, you will miss it. You are paying complete attention to the Now.

The Quietness of Your Presence Gives Rise to Beauty

When you are still and present, it comes with a lot of peace. It is only then that you have the ability to appreciate the magnificent beauty of nature. You will listen and notice. This will also enable the internal spirit to unfold easily. We experience such moments at times and these are the moments of no-mind.

We do not even notice such moments at times since the gap between such moments and the entry of thought might be too slim. When this gap between thought and observation becomes broader, it adds depth to you as a human being. If we cannot stay still, we will be unable to truly appreciate the beauty of nature.

Attaining Pure Consciousness

When we become conscious of Being, Being becomes conscious of itself. The latter is presence. However, we should avoid trying to comprehend all the terminologies since we do not need to comprehend anything before becoming present.

Pure Consciousness

When consciousness finds freedom from its identification with physical and mental forms, it acquires the status of pure or enlightened consciousness. This is also known as presence. Very few people are able to release themselves from their mind. If we do not free ourselves from our egoic mind, we are doomed. It will lead to confusion and fear.

Jesus Christ and Pure Consciousness

The man Jesus became Christ, a vessel for pure consciousness. We need to comprehend our innate ability to recognize divinity. Avoid trying to customize Christ. Avoid turning him into a form identity.

If you feel pulled toward an enlightened teacher, it means that you already have sufficient presence to identify presence in another person. Some people do not feel pulled to the likes of Jesus and Buddha. Darkness cannot identify light. Egos are pulled to even greater egos. You can also benefit from group work to strengthen the illumination of your presence.

Key Lesson

When you become alert and wait for your next thought, it will not come easily. Being present kills thoughts. Powerful presence gives you freedom from thought. You are still and alert. It blocks mental noise. You let your guard down and it appears again.

Be strongly engrained within yourself.

Chapter 6: The Body Inside

Your Deepest Self is Actually Being

We need to have deep foundations within ourselves because our body can serve as a portal into the territory of Being. You can feel Being as the always present 'I am' that surpasses name and form. Feeling and being aware that you are and standing in that strongly embedded state is enlightenment and the truth according to Jesus that will set us free.

Freedom

We might question as to what this freedom is. This is freedom from the delusion that we do not exist beyond our physical body and mind. This is freedom from the never-ending fear that results from our belief in our existence as only in these forms. It also means freedom from sin since we impose it on ourselves in the form of suffering, resulting from our belief in these forms, which control our thoughts, words and actions.

Discover Your Hidden and Imperishable Reality

Our body, which is visible to us and we can touch, cannot transport us to Being. However, it is only the outer layer of something more multidimensional. Your natural state of linking with Being can enable you to feel this more profound reality as the hidden internal body. It is the enlivening presence inside us. Dwelling in the body means feeling it from within, feeling the existence inside the body and realizing that your existence surpasses the outer shell.

However, this is only the start of your journey. It will take you inside a place of unmatched peace and quietness. It also leads to wonderful power and effervescence. You can only experience moments of it initially. You will learn that you are not useless. Your inside is linked with something bigger and remarkable. Your mind does not let you see it.

Linking with the Inside Body

Close your eyes. You need it now but will not need it later when it will have become easy for you to be in the body. Channel your attention into the body. Feel it from inside. Do you feel the life in it? Do you feel life in your hands, arms, feet, chest and abdomen? Can you feel the subtle energy field all over your body? Keep concentrating on your inner body for some time. Feel it and do not think about it. You will feel each cell becoming more alive. The feeling of your inner body does not have a limit or form. You cannot comprehend it. Feel whatever you can. You can go deeply later.

The Body as the Vessel of Transformation

No one can become enlightened by rejecting or battling their body. The body is where core transformation happens.

Deeper Roots Inside

Stay eternally linked with your inner body. Feel it all the time. This will keep getting deeper quickly and change your life. When you keep channeling more consciousness into your inner body, its vibrational frequency will keep multiplying. When you attain this greater energy level, negativity will not be able to leave an effect on you anymore.

Forgive before You Get Inside

It might be difficult for many of us to enter our inner body initially. We do not need to think about it. We only need to feel it. Feel the emotion. If you find blame or bitterness, it might mean that you have not forgiven yourself, someone else, or a situation for something. When you forgive, you take away power from your mind. You can be present now and enter your inner body.

Our Link with the Unmanifested

Presence is another name for pure consciousness. The inner body is our connection with the Unmanifested and equals the Unmanifested in its deepest element. The Unmanifested is the Source/root from which consciousness springs. Cognizance of the inner body is consciousness recalling its roots and going back to the source.

The Unmanifested is another word for Being.

Benefits of Awareness of the Inner Body

The several advantages of being aware of the inner body include decelerating the aging process, firming up the immune system, and several others.

Use Breathing to Establish a Link with Your Inner Body

If you cannot detach yourself from your mind, utilize conscious breathing to initiate a connection with your inner body.

How to Use the Mind Creatively

When you need to utilize your mind for a particular objective, use it in unification with your inner body. You can utilize your mind creatively minus conscious thought. You can enter that state by utilizing your body. When you require a creative idea, a solution or an answer, halt thinking and concentrate on your inner energy field. Be alert to the motionlessness. When you go back to thinking, it will be creative and fresh.

How to Listen to Other People

When you listen to other people, listen with your entire body instead of your mind only. While listening, experience the energy field of your inner body. It will deviate from thinking and let you listen without interruption from the mind.

Key Lesson

You need to take away consciousness from your mind to become conscious of Being.

Chapter 7: Portals into the Unmanifested

Going Further into the Body

If you can enter your body but cannot go any deeper, turn it into a meditation. Ten to fifteen minutes will be enough. Avoid any distractions including people and phones. Sit on a chair but keep your spine straight. It will help you stay alert. You can also select your own preferred position for meditation.

Keep your body relaxed. Close your eyes. Take some deep breaths. Feel yourself breathing into the lower portion of your abdomen. Watch how it expands and contracts with every single breath. Then notice the whole energy field of the body. Feel it. This is how you recoup consciousness from the mind.

The Source of Chi

Chi is known in the East as a type of universal life energy. The Unmanifested is not Chi; it the source of Chi. Chi is the inner energy field of our body. It serves as a passage between the Source and our outer shell. It is in the middle of the Unmanifested and the manifested i.e. the universe of form.

Dreamless Sleep is a Portal

When we experience deep dreamless sleep at night, it takes us into the Unmanifested. We connect with the Source. We take core energy from it to help us when we come back to the universe of the manifested. The Unmanifested cannot set us free if we do not enter it consciously.

Other Portals

The Now is the primary portal. It is a fundamental element of every single portal, including the inner body. We will be unable to enter our body without being truly present in the Now. Time and the manifested have a strong link, just like the timeless Now and the Unmanifested.

When we stop thinking by taking a conscious breath or observing a flower while being powerfully attentive, without any thoughts, it gives rise to another portal. One more portal comes alive when we succumb and set the inner mental - emotional resistance free to what is. Love is not a portal.

Another portal is silence. Pay heed to outer silence and inner silence will follow. A portal will open. Space, from within and without, also serves as a portal.

The Reality of Space and Time

Nothing could exist without space. The space in the universe is a reflection of the Unmanifested. Space and time are the two fundamental attributes of God, infinity and eternity.

Conscious Death

People who have had near-death experiences have underlined a portal opening in the form of glowing light. This unintentional portal opens for a limited time when physical death happens. This portal opens right after the death of a body.

Key Lesson

If you feel unable to go deeper into your body, use meditation.

Chapter 8: Bringing Enlightenment into Relationships

Embrace the Now from Your Current Position, Regardless of Where It Is

Some people believe that true enlightenment only occurs through love between a man and a woman. However, this is false. True enlightenment has to happen here and now.

A lot of people seek physical or psychological gratification. They believe that such things will bring happiness or fulfillment to them. However, real salvation is another name for peace, contentment and life in its completeness. It equals being oneself, feeling the good one has without any contradictions, and the delight of Being that has no external dependencies. This refers to the act of knowing God as your deepest essence. None of your actions or achievements can bring you as close to salvation as the present moment.

Relationships that Fluctuate between Love and Hate

Without the consciousness regularity of presence, all relationships, and especially intimate relationships, are quite defective and dysfunctional. They seem to be great in the start, when people are 'in love.' However, it does not last forever when clashes, arguments, discontent, and emotional or physical aggression rear their head. A majority of love relationships turn into love/hate connections after some time. They fluctuate between the two emotions and give us both happiness and sorrow. People even become hooked to such cycles. If one partner leaves, the other one becomes aggressive.

The Quest for Completeness and Addiction

Why Do People Get So Addicted to the Other Person in Love?

People chase and get addicted in love and romantic relationships are so popular because it gives people freedom from a deep-rooted fear of incompleteness and a need that are characteristic of humans when they have not attained enlightenment.

A man yearns for a woman and a woman craves a man because they are both incomplete and two parts of a whole. This is why sexual unification is so satisfying and the closest thing to completeness on a physical level. However, sexual unification is just an instant of ecstasy and a glance at completeness.

The sense of incompleteness or dearth on a psychological level is even stronger than it is on a physical level. When you identify with your mind, your ego is always pursuing completeness. However, when a special relationship happens, it appears to be a solution to all issues experienced by the ego and all its expectations. The things that contributed to your sense of self before do not seem to matter now. Your loved one becomes your point of focus and your world revolves around him or her. Do the feelings of incompleteness go away or do they get concealed below the surface?

If you love your partner one instant and attack them the next, it is not love. It is just a way for your ego to find fulfillment. Each addiction results from an unconscious denial to face and navigate through your pain. Each addiction begins and ends with pain. This is the case with intimate relationships. They bring so much pain after the early ecstasy because they serve as addictions. Also, they do not give birth to pain. They only bring the pain and unhappiness inside us to the surface.

This is why people do not want to live in the Now. They do not want to face their pain. Evading relationships is not a solution either because failed relationships might also help you reach enlightenment.

How to Change an Addictive Relationship into an Enlightened One?

We can change an addictive relationship into an enlightened one by staying present and adding strength to that presence by focusing our attention powerfully into the Now. This works whether you are alone or with a partner.

Love equals a state of Being. It resides within you and can never leave you.

Relationships and Spirituality

If there are issues in your relationship, just being aware of and acknowledging them can make a huge difference. Your knowing can change your turmoil into peace. You cannot transform yourself or your partner when it comes to inner transformation. You can only prepare a space for it.

If your relationship makes you crazy and is not functioning, treat it as an opportunity for salvation. However, if you chase salvation through a relationship, it will not happen. If you embrace the idea that the relationship will make you conscious rather than happy, then you will achieve salvation. It will also help you synchronize with a higher consciousness.

Women and the Pain-body

Women are closer to enlightenment than men because men are more inclined toward the thinking mind. What impedes women from accomplishing enlightenment is their pain-body.

Women experience the collective pain-body individually because of emotional pain experienced in the past. The collective pain-body of women is part of their overall psyche, because of thousands of years of suppression by men, abuse, rape, and so on. The pain-body becomes more pronounced during menstruation. When women rise beyond the pain-body, they become enlightened.

Women can only take control of the pain-body by becoming conscious of it. When you astonishingly realize that you have been connected to your pain, you break your link with it. Avoid utilizing the pain-body to offer yourself an identity. Utilize it for enlightenment.

Key Lesson

If you seek salvation through a relationship, it will be futile. If you accept that the relationship will make you conscious and not blissful, then you will gain salvation. It will also harmonize you with a greater level of consciousness.

Chapter 9: Peace beyond Joy and Sorrow

The Difference between Happiness and Inner Peace

Inner peace does not rely on conditions being supposed to be positive. Happiness does.

Is It Possible to Know What is Positive?

We might think that if we stay completely positive, we will pull only positive events and occurrences toward us. However, it does not work like that since we cannot be sure what is positive and what is negative. A lot of people have found pain, disease, loss, failure or restraint as their most impactful teacher. It helped them get rid of shallow ego-directed goals and wants and inaccurate self-images. When something negative happens in your life, it comes with a lesson beneath it. When you observe from a higher perspective, conditions are always positive.

It does not mean that you are imagining something negative to be positive. You are just letting it be. If you can change something about such a situation, change it while letting it be.

Your Life Drama Comes to a Halt

When you have achieved acceptance and inner peace that way, something might happen that might seem 'bad' from the viewpoint of ordinary consciousness. A majority of the bad things that occur in people's lives stem from unconsciousness. What gives rise to them is self or ego. These things can be known as 'drama.' Drama does not happen in the life of conscious people. You will not experience any clashes with yourself and others when conflict ceases to exist between your demands and what actually is.

Cycles of Life and Change

Nothing lasts forever. Even if you achieve consciousness, you might experience pain. Do not label it as suffering. There will be cycles of success and failure both in life. The cycles of the universe are powerfully tangled with the temporariness of every situation and thing. According to the Buddha, our happiness and unhappiness are the same thing. They are split by an illusion of time.

Getting Rid of Negativity

Every instance of negativity is resistance. The ego considers something to be manipulated so that it can get what it wants from it. Avoid resistance and negativity. Succumb to the Now.

A repetitive negative emotion like depression might be an indicator that something is wrong with your life and you need to make some changes. However, a change will only make a difference if it stems from a modification in your consciousness level. So, be present first. You can create a barrier to negativity by being completely present.

Having Compassion

When you become detached from your mind and present in the Now, you become compassionate to others. When you become closely linked with Being, you will be able to recognize the actual reality of people, just like your own. You will be able to handle other people's unconscious behavior or suffering by staying present and linked with Being. You will be able to experience their pure Being through your own.

Key Lesson

Avoid resistance and negativity by being present. Succumb to the Now.

Chapter 10: What Does It Mean by Surrender?

Embrace the Now

Surrendering to the Now does not mean that we should not try to make things better. Surrendering does not mean something negative. We should make plans and take positive actions all the time. We should try to improve our situations. Surrender refers to the insightful wisdom of life, which means softening to instead of resisting the flow of life. If you cannot put up with a situation in your life, you can only handle it by surrendering to it first to stop the unconscious resistance outline surrounding it.

Mind Energy Turns into Spiritual Energy

We can get rid of resistance by starting with admitting it. Stay there when the resistance rears its head. Watch how your mind gives rise to and tags it. When you observe it, you will realize that it does not lead to any good. You will turn the unconscious resistance into something conscious by concentrating your energy into the Now. This will kill the resistance.

Even if a person is ill, surrendering means accepting the situation. It does not mean losing the will to fight or live. Surrender to your suffering, grief, sorrow and sadness. Turn it into peace.

The Lack of Choice

None of us like suffering or dysfunction. They arise because we hold on to past pain. We need to comprehend that when people are run by their mind, they do not realize that they are doing anything wrong. It is a dysfunctional state. However, even if people who are controlled by their mind do not realize what they are doing wrong, they will have to bear the consequences.

Forgiveness and the Now

A lot of us do not actually comprehend forgiveness. If we keep holding on to the past, we can neither forgive ourselves nor others completely. We can only truly forgive by embracing the Now. You will understand that none of your own past actions or things done to you by others can trace your real essence. When you succumb to what is and become completely present, the past will stop having any power. Now is the answer.

You will know you have succumbed when you do not ask this question anymore.

Key Lesson

Surrender to the Now. It does not mean you cannot take positive action. Do that and try to improve the situations faced by yourself. However, do not resist.

Conclusion

Most of us are just living our lives by serving as our mind's slaves. We do not question our thoughts at all and spend our lives in a state of unconsciousness. Pain and suffering engulf us and our thoughts bother us. Our mind does not let us have a moment of peace. Eckhart Tolle teaches us in *The Power of Now* that we can take away the reins from our mind. We can surrender to the present and become conscious. We can improve our existence by letting go of thought and find peace. Most importantly, by being present, we can let the past and future go and focus on the Now to connect with Being and the purpose of our lives.

Made in the USA
Monee, IL
12 February 2020